# SHADES

MIA HEINTZELMAN

LeviLynn
BOOKS

Copyright©2018 by Mia Heintzelman

Library of Congress Cataloging-in-Publication Data
Names: Heintzelman, Mia, author
Title: Shades / Mia Heintzelman.
Description: First Edition. | Las Vegas: Levi Lynn Books, 2018.
ISBN-13: 978-0-9990493-2-7 | ISBN-10: 0-9990493-2-1

Cover Design and illustration by dot covers

# CONTENTS

## LIGHT

## BLINDED

## BRILLIANT

## FADE

## OBSCURE

# DARKNESS

# BLACKNESS

# LIGHT

# ETHEREALITY

SUNLIGHT THROUGH TREES
WATER TURNS TO ICE
I'M EXPERIENCING SPIRITUALITY UNFILTERED

AS I BEND DOWN ON MY KNEES TO GIVE THANKS
I'M HERE AT THE BANKS THE SHORE WHERE OUR FOOTPRINTS ONCE MET

IN THIS PLACE, IT'S WHERE SOLITUDE DOES NOT MEAN LONELINESS
I'M JUST LIFTED

RATHER, I'M ON A PEDESTAL
RISING TO HIS DIVINE ORDER
SPEAKING UP FOR REDEMPTION
BENDING MY HEAD DOWN IN PRAYER
BECAUSE I KNOW HE'S THERE LINGERING

IN MY SOUL
IN MY LAIR

I KNOW HE'S THERE
I'M EXPERIENCING SPIRITUALITY ETHEREALLY

# KINDRED SOUL

IN YOUR EYES
I SEE STRENGTH AMONG THE GREATEST ADVERSITY
IN YOUR EYES
I SEE POSSIBILITY AMIDST IMPOSSIBILITY
IN YOUR EYES
A WINDOW OPENS AND ALAS I CAN SEE

IN YOUR SOUL
I HEAR THE SOUND OF MY HEART AS I'M FILLED WITH PRIDE BRIMMING AT
THE SEAMS
IN YOUR SOUL
I HEAR DREAMS REDEFINING REALITY
IN YOUR SOUL
A DOOR OPENS, SILENCE HALTS, AND ALAS I CAN HEAR

WITH YOU
I SPEAK WITH DIGNITY AND RIGHTEOUSNESS
WITH YOU
I SPEAK ABOUT A WORLD THAT HAS TO GIVE WAY TO THE MARK OF A NEW
HISTORY
WITH YOU

I SPEAK FORMIDABLY WITH A PRESENCE THAT CANNOT BE PERMITTED BUT COMMANDED

FOR, WITH YOU
WITH EACH GLIMMER IN YOUR EYE, WHISPER IN YOUR SOUL, AND GLIMPSE OF WISDOM YOU SPEAK
A NEWNESS EMERGES URGENTLY

FOR, IN YOU
I AM GRACED WITH THE GIFT OF CLEARLY SEEING ME.

# MY FRIEND AND MY LOVE

As time grows long and feelings grow strong
May loneliness never befall you

As some times prove bad and your mood tends to be sad
May you remember that you always have a friend in me

You are my love and my friend
Though heartbreak and heartache
Through tears and fears
Through distance and barriers
Because God continues to carry us

You will always be dear to my heart and present in my soul
Through trials and tribulations
Bliss and revelations
Past and future
Solid and whole
There's no one who knows me better

There's no one with whom I want to share more
You are my friend and my love

# VOW

I'VE WAITED MY WHOLE LIFE TO MEET YOU
WE'VE CROSSED PATHS MANY TIMES IN MY HEART, SOUL, AND DREAMS

NOW ON THIS DAY, I'M WHOLLY COMPLETE NOW THAT YOU'VE ARRIVED
NOW THAT YOU ARE HERE
NOW THAT YOU ARE MINE

NOW, I KNOW AND TRUST IN MY LORD FURTHER BECAUSE I AM BLESSED
HE MADE ME ON PURPOSE FOR A PURPOSE
AND THAT PURPOSE IS TO LOVE AND BE LOVED BY YOU

YOU WERE THAT ANGEL JUST BEYOND THE CLOUDS
NOW YOU ARE MY ANGEL WITH WHOM I SHARE THIS HAVEN AND THIS
EMBRACE

I LOVE YOU WITH ALL THAT I AM
I LOVED YOU BEFORE I MET YOU
I LOVE YOU FOR THE MAN THAT YOU ARE NOW

TO ME LIFE HAS JUST BEGUN
BECAUSE YOU WERE MY DREAM AND NOW YOU ARE REAL
I LOVE YOU

# BLINDED

# FROM WITHIN

Sometimes as I stare through the glass
I hear pebbles being thrown at the window upon my balcony
Beckoning my company

And I enthusiastically answer
With joy in my tone
Because I never did care for being alone

And it is then
That I hear your voice
Bellowing through my soul

I feel your touch
Devouring me whole

And so I come down

To experience this conquest firsthand
As I obey your every command Just to take my chance at understanding
What it's like to look up at the world
From this angel's point of view

# GUIDED

When the lord looked down at me
Angels surrounded me

And showered me with the joy of love
It was under his praise
That I began to see the sunshine through the haze

I was glowing like light from halos
Indulging in everything that everyone in salvation undergoes
When the angels touched me with hands soft as water lilies
Suddenly my life was in bloom

And everything I had assumed would overcome me
Became heaven on earth

Life in the clouds
And eternal bliss
Overwhelming me

It was God's kiss

And as I walked those footprints just to see I looked up as the lord looked down at me

# MIRROR IMAGE

Please allow me to take you by the hand
I would like to deliver you from your fears
And take you to a place where comfort is your home

I would like to wrap you in my embrace
Stare into your face
And make it known what I am

I am within you
I am your inner self
I lie beyond the depths

In a sea of emotions
More vast than the oceans
Full of power and strength
I would go to the greatest length
To devour your inner fears
Make it known throughout your years

While I tempt temptations
And exceed your greatest expectations

Still you know not that I am here
That I am your fear
I am you out on the ledge
I am your mirror image

# WHAT LIES

Somehow intrigue enters the mind
An inquiry is all that lies

When it seems that all the questions have been answered
Mystery showers its plague upon the life that was once known
And again the unknown is all that lies

It's the sense of completion
It's the sense of closure
It's the sense of redemption
That the depth of the soul awaits

And still all that lies is the need
A void wide open
A festering wound

The departure of the day
It is what lies

# BRILLIANT

# AROMA

An aroma passed my nose
As if to beckon me into a certain direction

Silky and erotic
Stroking my senses into an erection
Arousing my thoughts
Leashing my soul
This flavor definitely took a toll

Looking over
I saw what could not be overlooked
Seeing all of what could not be overseen

I was feeling myself yearning for this find that I found
Craving the corruption of this creamy culprit
Who had stolen my self-control and willpower
And kidnapped my soul

Only thing was, I didn't want to be exonerated
I was content being captivated
By this masked malice
Who gave me shivers

AND OVERFLOWING RIVERS
TREMBLING QUAKES
AND CONTINUOUS SHAKES

GRABBING HOLD TO ALL THAT HANDS COULD HOLD
EXPERIENCING THINGS THAT I HAD ONLY BEEN TOLD
NO NEED FOR NEGOTIATION
THIS DEAL WAS ENVISIONED, BOUGHT, AND SOLD

AND AGAIN I CAUGHT A WHIFF OF THE AROMA
THAT OWNED ME
DEVOURED ME
AND EMPOWERED ME
AND LIFTED UP MY THRONE

OH THE SENSATION
OF NOT RESISTING THIS TEMPTATION
I FOUND PLEASURE IN THIS TREASURE
JEWELS PRICELESS

AS I BEGAN TO EXPERIENCE THE AROMA
ENGROSSED IN THIS SOMA
SO SOFT, SO SMOOTH
I WAS COMPLETELY FEELING THE PASSION IN THIS GROOVE
I WAS WHOLLY LEVELED WITH THE GLARE IN THAT STARE
I WAS HYPNOTIZED
TAKEN OVER
TAKEN UNDER
MOVED OVER
PUT IN A COMA
ALL BY THIS SIMPLE TEMPTING AROMA

# IN THE SPUR OF THE MOMENT

Oh, in the spur of the moment
A whole other place
A whole other state
Of mind and body
Where voice doesn't lie

The heart knows it well
While the brain is foreign
An exile, banished at this time
For the language of two hearts
Beating as one 'til the end

Its something logic can't comprehend
Reward centers booming and established
Stimulated, capitulated, unwilling to be exonerated
The sound of mating
Moans and groans
The agitated erogenous zones
Devouring mind, body, and souls

Some believe it's an omen
Considering the things that happen

IN THE SPUR OF THE MOMENT

HELPLESS AND POWERFUL
WEAK AND STRONG
NO THOUGHT JUST ACTION
SEEKING TO PLEASE
AND BE PLEASED
WHETHER STRAIGHTFORWARD OR TEASED
THIS IS IMPROMPTU
WHAT'S GOING ON WITH YOU?

OUT OF YOUR MIND
IN THE WRONG MIND
CONVINCED OF BEING IN THE RIGHT MIND
THINKING YOU FOUND YOUR FIND

IN AN INSTANT OF TIME
THIS IS INDECISION
IT'S PRECISION
A BOMBARDMENT
A COLLISION
OF BODIES AND IDEAS
HORMONES AND APPEALS
NEEDS AND DESIRES
CHEMISTRY AND FIRES

ERUPTING
IT'S CORRUPTING
YOUR MIND, BODY, AND SOUL
BECAUSE YOU'RE LOSING CONTROL
YOU'RE OUT OF CONTROL
ON A ROLL
UNAWARE OF THE TOLL
YOU'VE JUST SIGNED OVER YOUR SOUL

IT INVOLVES YOUR ENTIRE COMPONENT
ALL IN THE SPUR OF THE MOMENT

# LAVENDER LILACS

Picture with your mind
Imagine with your soul
All of the sounds of silence
That no one else seems to know

Hearing infinite decibels
Feeling all the passion of a million jezebels
Overwhelming you until you relax

Imagine lying in fields of lavender lilacs
Time stands still
While your imagination runs wild
Dreaming amongst the clouds
About life's treasures

Thinking aloud
About satisfying pleasures
And when you feel yourself straying off the tracks
Once again you wake up...
In a luminous field of lavender lilacs

# THE ROOT

You are the root to the flowering tree
The wellspring to our beautiful leaves
Thick and hard
Growing downward into the soil, Phenom who believes

You are the footing in a line of first steps
The milestone to a mountain embedded underground
Essential, fundamental
Our original true home, lost and found

You are the scion
The sway in our curves and the vigor in our voices
Thunder and lightning
Coursing with passion and conviction, with rhythm she rejoices

Beneath our soles
The crux, the bedrock
The square root
Turned over
Absorbed
Unearthed

You are the root to our flowering tree
The footing in our line of first steps
The scion and the source
You are us and we are you
For you gave us life and we are rooted in you

# FADE

# ENDING TO BEGINNING

THE LOVE I HAD FOR YOU HAS BEEN DRAINED FROM MY SOUL
SUCH A TREACHEROUS POISON HAS ESCAPED ME

DROP BY DROP IT SEEPED OUT OF MY PORES

ONLY TO BE EVAPORATED BY THE SUN
INTO THIN AIR MY PAIN HAS GONE
AND SO I KNOW IT'S A NEW DAY
AND LIFE HAS JUST BEGUN

# SUCCUMB

I'VE GOT LOVE ON MY MIND
I'VE GOT LOVE IN MY HEAD
IT'S YOU PERMEATING ME

MY THOUGHTS
MY WORDS MY AIR

SURROUNDING ME IN ESSENCE

IT'S YOUR PRESENCE
IT'S TAKEN ITS TOLL ON ME
ALL I WANT IS YOU

# SUMMER SET

On days when the sun is still
And the night sneaks in before dark
Heat waves farewell
And wind blows me kisses
Whispering sweet nothings that are truly something

In the distance, the trees bark
Providing shelter and shade a home to return to

The animals call in the wild
Greetings of goodwill
Blessings of nature's best company

The sky leans down and hugs its sun
And wind whistles a sweet lullaby before sleep

Only in these summer slumber parties
When Sol is sleep and Luna comes out to play
Does she shine so bright

Flashing the world's stars her pearly whites
Amongst the sweet oranges and somber blues of the stage set

ON DAYS WHEN THE SUN IS STILL

AND THE NIGHT SNEAKS IN BEFORE DARK

HEAT WAVES FAREWELL

AND WIND BLOWS ME KISSES

WHISPERING SWEET NOTHINGS THAT ARE TRULY SOMETHING

# SUNRISE, SUNDOWN, AND DAWN

AND WHEN THE NIGHT FALLS
I WILL BE THERE TO CATCH IT

SIMPLY ON THE TERMS THAT I AM ONE WITH IT
ENGULFED IN THE DARKNESS
ENGAGED IN THE MYSTERY
YET CLEAR AS WATER

NURTURING TO ITS OFFSPRING STARS
AND PARTIAL TO ITS MOON

AND WHEN THE DAY RISES
I WILL BE ALONG ITS SIDE SOARING
DARING TO BE EXPLORING
AS THE BRIGHT LIGHT SPARKLES ITS GLITTER OF DAY UPON ME

I WILL SPARKLE LIKE THE TWINKLE IN THE SUN'S EYE
AND STILL MY GLIMMER SPREADS LIKE CONTAGION TO THOSE AROUND ME
BECAUSE I AM LIKE TO THE LIVING
AND I PROVIDE THE VIBRANT COLOR IN THE TREES AND GRASS

AND WHEN PEOPLE SMILE IT'S MY SHINE THAT HAS GONE THE EXTRA MILE

It is fortunate that this cycle of brilliance replicates itself
So that I may imitate its stealth

Sunrise, sundown, and dawn
Creating a new spawn of life and magnificence

And the day begins again
And so, I shall rise again

# OBSCURE

# AND THINGS MAY CHANGE

And things may change
Because that is constant

And we too may change
Still we will remain constant

Continuing on as parts of our lives
Sharing times and memories
Despite our lives and what the future reads

So I urge you to peer into the sands of time
As each grain becomes one with the hour glass
Reaching destinies of what's to be
Exploring fates of what awaits

And though things may change
They will still remain the same
As will we

# CLIMB UP

I'M ON THE CLIMB
BOOSTING
BOUNDLESS
ON MY WAY UP

ALL THE WAY UP
ALL THE WAY UP

I HEAR THE BEAT
POUNDING IN MY HEAD

I'M INVINCIBLE
BIG DREAMS
DREAMS IN COLOR
RAINBOW IN THE SKY

BUTTERFLY IN THE SKY
I CAN FLY TWICE AS HIGH

ALL THE WAY UP
UP WAY THE ALL
EITHER WAY YOU LOOK AT IT

Up against the fall

I'm on the climb
Striving
Endless
Pushing my way up

Focused
Zoomed in
Fired up

On the come up
All the way up
I'm on the climb

# GIVE AND TAKE

You got me to open up my eyes
You made me see through another lens
You put happiness within my view
But then you disappeared from my sight

You got me to open up my heart
You taught me about my emotions and feelings
You gave me joy with every heartbeat
But then you refused my heart when I tried to give it to you

You tried when I was stubborn
You praised me when I was down
You gave me a push when I couldn't start
But then when I got started you abandoned me and left me all alone

You gave and we started
You waved and we parted
I still had faith it could all be renewed
Isn't there a way we can start off where we finished?

# SORRY-ISH

I'M SO HAPPY FOR YOU
...KIND OF
EXCEPT FOR THE FACT THAT I CAN'T BRING MYSELF TO ACTUALLY BE

YOUR HAPPINESS AND YOUR SUCCESS
SOMEHOW MOUNT MY STRESS
MAKING ME FEEL LESS, MORE OR LESS

I WOULD RATHER SEVER TIES
I WOULD RATHER SPREAD LIES
PRAY ON YOUR PAIN
RATHER THAN HAVE YOUR BLESSING WEIGHING ON MY BRAIN

I'VE BEEN SLACKING
UNPACKING
MY BAGGAGE AND THE WRONGS THAT MIGHT MAKE THINGS BETWEEN US
RIGHT

I WANT TO BE HAPPY FOR YOU
I WANT TO ROOT AND CHEER
LET'S POP THE CHAMPAGNE AND CELEBRATE
IF ONLY I COULD DISCOUNT THIS HATE

I HATE TO DIM YOUR FLAME
SHAME, SHAME, SHAME
I HATE TO LOOK DOWN UPON YOUR NAME

I WANT TO BE SO HAPPY FOR YOU
I'M SORRY
SO, SO, SO SORRY
...KIND OF

# DARKNESS

# DEPTH

Deep, breathe
I inhale you
And feel you seep into my veins

Running through me
You provide me with life
Air into my dreams
Hope flowing straight into my heart
Palpitating love to my mind
I found my find

Lurking near
All I see and hear
Thinking, deep
To my dismay, I'm still asleep

Dreaming my dream
Behind my closed windows is where you live
Love you live here
Sweet slumber, take me back into the darkness of deep

# DYING DAY

The day died
And somehow I was stuck in an eternal night
Ironically enough the night remained light

I thought that I would live in the dim glim of the lover's din
But I had been through that valley again and again

I was reaching new peaks
And allowing myself to imagine
Life on stars, like diamond drops
Gleaming their intensity
And exceeding the sky's limit

My glare overwhelmed the moon
And the thickness of life
Dominated the misty dew
And at that moment when the day died

I did not mourn the morning
Rather I welcomed the eve of the evening
And danced in the midst of stardust

I LIT THE FIRE OF THE LANTERN MOON
AND WATCHED ITS SPARKS BREATH THE BLAZE INTO FIREFLIES
LEAVING ME PARTNERS WITH WHOM TO DANCE

AS THE NIGHT GLISTENED WE MADE WAVES OF SATIN RIBBONS
AND WATCHED THE ANGELS SWAY
LIKE HEATHER ON HILLS
WITH RHYTHM LIKE THE CURRENT OF WHITE RIVERS FLOWING EXACTLY
WHERE THEY'RE GOING
AND AS THE DAY DIED, LIFE WE SET, AS THE SUN SET

# FEMME NOIR

Black woman
You are me, and I am you
I am so much more than the 3/5 of a person we were once claimed
to be

Though I am lighter in shade than your ebony hue
I am nonetheless one with you

Full of life
Exuberant and real
Engorged with passion
Permeating my seams

Strong in so many senses
From holding a world and history on my shoulders
From leaning to lift others as I rise

Yes, my neck rolls from rage
And my behind can be described by the shapes of apples and onions

I am the epitome of an angry black woman
I am a mad black woman...

When I need to be

Because I defend my loved ones and my honor endlessly?
But anger doesn't encompass my soul
It runs deep and complex
Beyond words and circumstances

My soul loves and longs to be loved
I am to be cherished and appreciated
Mutually and unconditionally
And while it will never be easy to love me

The love I give will be the greatest home for your heart

# UNSUNG LOVE

THERE'S NOTHING QUITE LIKE UNREQUITED LOVE
ONE GIVES ALL OF HER LOVE
THE OTHER NOT QUITE THE SAME SUM

I'M IN LOVE WITH YOU
I LOVE YOU, BUT I'M NOT IN LOVE WITH YOU

NOTHING ELSE HAS THAT STING
WHEN YOU KNOW THE LOVE YOU HAVE IS ONLY A THING

NOT MUCH, NOT ENOUGH, NOT QUITE
OUT OF REACH
OUT OF SIGHT
NOT WORTH GIVING
NOT WORTH TIME
NOT OF WORTH
NOT QUITE

# UNTIL SUMMER

I think I knew you all along

For years I saw you in passing
But we never met until summer

My mind recognized you before my eyes could get a glimpse
I'm sure it was you, but it never made sense

Always close by, but just out of reach
It was smoke and mirrors really
Ethereally sashaying across my mind
A lingering reminder of your presence yet to come

The blossoms of spring left footprints in the sand
The antecedent of the inevitable

Awaiting, for years I saw you in passing
But still, we never met until summer

The fog lifted and it dawned on me

By chance, we had stolen silent moments alone amongst droves of bystanders
Under the blazing of the day, a spark nudged you into plain view

Enamored, the sun warmed us
As you sat engrossed in the works of written words
Finally, I was seeing you beyond the measure of what was

You are what it is
My mind recognized you and my indifferent eyes took notice
Now impassioned, I know you, and it makes sense
Somehow you're up close, and divinely just within reach
Your alluring charm captured me
Ignited with a renewed fervor to explore the esoteric possibilities of what if
I ascribe my ardent desire to indulge in life without limits to your presence

I knew you all along

For years I was getting to know you in passing
Without precedence

Beyond the shadow of a doubt

Irrevocably, the time to reveille came
When summer summoned us

# WITHERING RIBBONS

Hope faded like faith
Souls jaded like man
Into thin air ribbons start to wither

Red white and blue
Colors in the land of the free
Screaming for mercy Yet silenced by time

Emotions in the midst
Tarnishing the love of kin
Siblings in the human race
Blinded by individual gain

Red white and blue
Colors in the home of the brave
Cowered by shame
News mimicking life
Or life mimicking the news

Civilization's confused
Adopting the views
That two wrongs make a right

Red white and blue
Colors of the withering ribbons
Waiting for the resuscitation of this nation
Waiting to wave again
Not in vain
Not in haste
For the free, for the brave, for the human race

# BLACKNESS

# IT'S YOUR WORLD

Relaxed, natural, dreaded, afro
Home grown or store bought, it's yours

Caramel, yellow, pale, chocolate, ebony
Girl you've got that glow

Snap 'em, slap 'em, hit 'em, high five
Give yourself a hand

Slim, tall, short, thick, petite, big-boned
Shake it, but don't break it

With your rhythm and blues, and bohemian grooves
It's all in the way you move

Never be ashamed of your unique beauty
Black is Black

And Black is Beautiful
Sister girl
Anyway you play
It's your world

# KNEEL TO STAND

They say that when the world ends
There will be catastrophe and chaos

Mountains crumbling to the sea
Violence and war
Violence and hate
Turmoil and strife
Hurricanes and floods
Remnants of a black and blue fight

It isn't in my blood

Commander, we got beef
Mishandler in chief
Liar, we need relief

You are the leader of the un-free world
A button-pusher
Unfiltered
Shock jock
Ticking time clock

Liar, liar, we need you to retire
You operate on sound bites and tweets
Controversy and deceit

Tourette syndrome
Tweeting like nervous tics
Unwanted movements
Insecure
Deplorable

You got my head hot
Hand dipped in every pot
But I don't need you to grab me by the...

Aha. Caught you
Hold up a mirror

Cower, coward
You'll still have your money and power

You've started a revolution
Your exit is our solution

You drudged all this up
Drudged up all this sin
The world is coming to an end

Purpose
Matter
Lives
With my pen, I'm a baller kneeling to take a stand

Please kneel
So that this world will stand

# WHAT TO DO WITH IT

Get over it
Get under it
It's beyond you
Though it's all around you

You're above it
Get in or out of it
Make the choice upon it
You're within it It's not beneath you
You're getting nearer
Though you're still quite far

Fall into it
It's only love

# SHADES

It perturbs me

I mean, it really deeply disturbs me
That when I smile at you on the street
I get looks as hard as concrete

Black power Black is beautiful
But if the juice is sweeter when the berry is blacker
Does that mean my juice is sour?

My berry isn't that dark, but I'm still sweet
When I walk into a room full of my strong black sisters
The only welcome I get comes straight from your misters

I missed your pearly whites
I must have been blinded by your stares, gleams, and glares

You had to see my hairstyle
You had to see what shoes I wore
You had to interrogate my essence
Before you could acknowledge my presence

My eyes are green... I sing in the likeness of Baduism
But I'm not the bandit
Either my yellow skin is too bright or it's too pale
But I'm not the reason you're still waiting to exhale

Instead of welcoming me as one of your own
I got the cold shoulder
The eye roll
You blew the whistle
All the cues of your dismissal

Breathe child and let that ego deflate
You've got way too many problems on your plate
Not enough love and too much hate

I hear about embracing the human race
I hear about evolving to a different place
With dignity and so-called grace
Is it that hard for you look at me with a smile on your face?

I'm not a Delta or an AKA
But I'm your soul sister anyway

It's not painful for me to accept you unconditionally
It would be nice to enter a room among you
And not have eyes cut in my direction
Like a knife severing our ties

Hearing, "she thinks she's so..." feel in the blank

Ask me what I think I am
I'm plain and simple, human
And coincidentally my eyes and skin are a little bit lighter and my hair is a little longer
But my feelings weigh in much stronger

I NEED YOU AROUND TO BE THAT STRONG BLACK WOMAN WITH ME
SOMETIMES, EVEN THAT ANGRY BLACK WOMAN WITH ME
BUT EVEN MORE, A WOMAN TO BE FRIENDS WITH ME
PERHAPS, JUST FRIENDLY WITH ME

# ALSO BY MIA HEINTZELMAN

**LOVE & GAMES SERIES**

ALL IS FAIR IN LOVE AND BOARD GAMES.

MONOPOLOVE

TRIVIALIZED PURSUIT

**TERMS & CONDITIONS SERIES**

LOVE AND LAW. KNOW THE RULES, THEN BREAK THEM.

THE FRIENDSHIP CONTRACT

**THE ALL MIXED UP SERIES**

THEY CAN'T IGNORE THE LOVE SIGNS POINTING ALL AROUND THEM.

MIXED SIGNALS

MIXED MATCH

MIXED EMOTIONS

ALL MIXED UP - THE SERIES

**HOLIDAY ROMANCES**

MISTLETOE. TWINKLE LIGHTS. ROMANTIC HOLIDAY NIGHTS.

MARRIED & BRIGHT

MINGLE ALL THE WAY

WRAPPED UP IN BEAU

COZY LITTLE CHRISTMAS

OLIVE & PEAR'S CHRISTMAS DETOUR

**WASTELANDS ACADEMY SERIES**

DEVASTATED

RUINED - COMING SOON

**w/a EMMALINE ZANTHI**

SEXY BWWM SHORT READS.

THE STACKS

THE BLUE GATE

# ABOUT MIA HEINTZELMAN

Mia Heintzelman is a polka-dot-wearing, horror movie lover, who always has a book and a to-do list in her purse. When she isn't busy writing fictional happily-ever-afters, she is likely reading, or playing board games and eating sweets with her husband and two children. She writes fun, unforgettable, more than just laughs romance about strong women and men with enough heart to fall for them.

**Let's Connect!**
**Website:** miaheintzelman.com

**Newsletter:** miaheintzelman.com/newsletter.html

**FB Reader Group:** Facebook.com/groups/2219575585012649/

instagram.com/miaheintzelmanauthor
twitter.com/miaheintzelman
facebook.com/miaheintzelmanauthor
bookbub.com/authors/miaheintzelman
goodreads.com/miaheintzelman
amazon.com/author/miaheintzelman

www.ingramcontent.com/pod-product-compliance
Lightning Source LLC
Chambersburg PA
CBHW060535030426
42337CB00021B/4277